Spirit Wars
The Prophet Versus The Witch

Kimberly Moses

Copyright © 2025 by Kimberly Moses

All rights reserved. No part of this publication may be reproduced, distributed or transmitted in any form or by any means, including photocopying, recording, or other electronic or mechanical methods, without the prior written permission of the publisher, except in the case of brief quotations embodied in critical reviews and certain other noncommercial uses permitted by copyright law. For mission requests, write to the publisher, addressed " Attention: Permissions Coordinator," at the address below.

Kimberly Moses/Rejoice Essential Publishing
PO BOX 512
Effingham, SC 29541
www.republishing.org

Spirit Wars/Kimberly Moses

ISBN-13: 979-8-3485-3230-7

TABLE OF CONTENTS

PREFACE..v
CHAPTER 1: It's All About The Blood..............1
CHAPTER 2: Cease And Desist..........................7
CHAPTER 3: How I Got My Power..................21
CHAPTER 4: How I Got My Anointing............31
CHAPTER 5: The Battle Begins.......................55
SALVATION..83
ABOUT THE AUTHOR....................................85

Preface

We are in a battle, whether you agree or not. There is light versus darkness (Ephesians 8:5-11) and the flesh versus the spirit (Galatians 5:16–17). For instance, light represents Jesus, and darkness represents demonic spirits. The flesh represents the soulish realm, consisting of the mind, will, and emotions. The spirit represents God's Holy Spirit. Each of these is contrary to each other. The spirit is willing, but the flesh is weak. We face challenges when we want to do right but end up doing wrong. I never realized how much of a spiritual battle we are in until, at an early age, I started getting attacked by demonic spirits. When I surrendered to Jesus, the demonic activity stopped. God gave me the idea for the book many years ago to highlight this battle. Much of what you will read are things that I have experienced. Welcome to *Spirit Wars: The Prophet Versus The Witch*.

CHAPTER 1

It's All About The Blood

Boom! Screech! Crash! The sound of cars crashing permeates the air, and the smell of burning rubber dominates as the drivers slam on the brakes and brace for impact. 5-Cross is notorious for frequent car crashes. It earned its name because five streets converge at a single point in the center. 5-Cross is where Palmetto Road, Skibo Street, Lafayette Street, and North Circle intersect.

A man driving a truck hauling a boat failed to slow down when traffic ahead of him slowed. He was on his way to Lake Murray to fish. As a result, he slammed into an SUV, which pushed forward into oncoming traffic and crashed into a sedan. Inside the SUV were a newlywed husband and wife, who had just finished a lovely meal at their favorite cafe. Inside the sedan was a mom with her two small children. They had just left the movie theater.

The couple in the SUV and the family inside the sedan all died on impact. However, the man driving the truck survived with only a few minor injuries. As the car accident occurred, some cars swerved to avoid a collision. Good Samaritans and witnesses to the tragic event risked their lives by pulling onto the side of the road, rushing over to the horrific scene of the accident, and dialing 911.

As they approached the cars involved, they saw the shattered glass on the road and how the cars were smushed. Airbags had deployed, making it difficult to see inside. However, as they pulled back the airbags, they were horrified to find the lifeless bodies inside the vehicles. One of the witnesses approached the man in the truck and asked if he was okay. He got out of his vehicle, stunned, unable to comprehend what had just happened. The driver wasn't drunk or texting while driving. He told the witness that his brakes hadn't worked properly and thought maybe the weight of the boat he was towing made it harder for him to stop. There was no earthly explanation for why the crash occurred. The people on the scene were unaware of the darkness lurking around them.

The dispatcher at the emergency call center received an influx of calls reporting the multi-car accident. Shortly after, a fire truck, several ambulances, and a few police officers arrived to provide assistance and secure the scene.

5-Cross just had its 20th crash in two years. It seemed like the devil had won another battle as more lives were lost in a senseless way. Fear hung thick in the air, and city officials were scratching their heads trying to develop a strategy for safer roads. During the town meeting last month, one of the new changes was to increase the interval of pedestrian walk time before the signal changes to slow down traffic.

In an apartment above a boutique overlooking the downtown area of a small Carolina town, Sonya Fuller sat on her balcony enjoying the sunset. On her lap was a book called *The Book of Shadows*. She was a beautiful mixed woman, with a Haitian and Black father and an Irish and European mother. Sonya's skin was a warm tan, and she had long, thick, flowing, curly black hair. Despite her outer beauty, she harbored a deep darkness within.

As Sonya gazed at the sunset set, she received a breaking news alert on her cellphone. ***"Fatal Crash, Five Dead at 5-Cross, Shuts Down Intersection."*** As she read the report, a twisted smile formed on her lips, and she felt a surge of joy.

Sonya: Yes! My spells are working! I'm going to get more powerful.

At that moment, Sonya went inside her studio apartment. She was focused on becoming a powerful goddess and didn't have time to invest in a relationship or date. As soon as she stepped over the threshold, a dark presence met her and overtook her. She felt the spirit enter her body and then lift. Immediately, she knew she had captured the souls at the intersection of 5-Cross.

A few nights earlier, Sonya had parked her car in front of the automotive parts store. It was around 3 am, and there wasn't any traffic on the road. The store was right across from 5-Cross. Sonya carried a vial of goat blood that she had prepared during a ritual earlier that day. She looked both ways before running across the street to make sure there was no incoming traffic. Then she stopped briefly at the center point of 5-Cross, where all the roads met, dumping the vial of blood on the road.

She called on the elements in the atmosphere and proclaimed that this spot on the road would result in many more fatalities. She envisioned multiple car pile-ups as she briefly meditated on what she desired. Knowing she couldn't stay in the road for long, she made it quick, ran back to her car, and drove back to her apartment.

As Sonya sought power, riches, and status, her demon guide instructed her on how to obtain them. Every month, she would go to 5-Cross to repeat the same ritual. She had no idea of the rude awakening that awaited her, which would make her question everything that she believed in.

CHAPTER 2

Cease And Desist

In the town hall meeting, Monique Taylor, a pretty Caucasian woman with a small frame, sat on the bench and listened as city officials discussed their budget and informed the public of their plans to make their city more effective. Monique had long brown hair and hazel eyes.

Councilwoman Nash: The biggest challenge is the monthly accidents at 5-Cross. School buses use that route, and if anything were to happen to those children, it would be a mass calamity that we aren't ready for. When will new stoplights and timers be installed?

Mayor: The Department of Transportation is scheduled to begin work later this evening.

Councilwoman Nash: Okay, great. That's a start toward making our community safer. What's next on the agenda?

Councilman Brown: The Affordable Rent Act. How can we offer more houses in our area?

Even though Monique Taylor was present in the meeting, her mind was a thousand miles away. Everything the council members discussed faded out. God had instructed her to go to the monthly town hall meetings. She knew that one day, the Lord would have her get more involved, but for now, she would stay in her comfort zone and sit in the back of the room. She believed God had ordered her steps there because she was mandated to pray for her city. Once, she had a vision that she would be running for city council, but she was in no rush to make it happen.

Sometimes, as she sat in the meetings, she would become grieved by all the injustices in her community. Through many hardships and trials, she developed a passion for prayer. As the meeting ended, she knew that much more needed to be done. While putting timers in for pedestrians and slowing down traffic would help, she discerned a spiritual battle at play. She felt an overwhelming burden to address it.

Monique went to her car and drove to Lake View Park. Here, she enjoyed sitting in her car and staring at the peaceful lake. She found the water relaxing and spent much time praying there.

Monique: Dear Heavenly Father, I repent of my sins and for the sins of my community. Have mercy on me and my city. People are dying, and this community is scared. We all have to drive through 5-Cross, and we can't allow fear to stop us. You haven't given us the spirit of fear, but of power, love, and a sound mind.

As Monique prayed, tears formed in the corner of her eyes. She remembered all the people her community had lost due to tragic events at that intersection. One of those who passed away was Ben Crawford, a popular football player at the high school. Monique had always had a crush on him, but they never dated because he had a girlfriend. Ben and Monique would say hello to each other in passing in the hallways at school or at a store in the community.

One day in 10th grade, Monique forgot her lunch and had no money. She sat down at the lunch table with the other kids. Noticing that Monique didn't have any food, Ben offered her some of his fries. They had graduated from high school five years ago. Most of her classmates were now working full-time jobs, had earned a college degree, or had started a family.

One day, Ben was riding on his motorcycle through the intersection at 5-Cross when someone ran a red light and collided with him. Ben was thrown several feet into the air and landed hard on his back. He suffered crushing injuries as his lower vertebrae shattered. His motorcycle was scraped up, and the front wheel was bent. Paramedics rushed to the scene and did their best to aid him. Despite their efforts to revive him, Ben died en route to the hospital. The community was in disarray when the news broke of Ben's passing last year. One of her old classmates came to Monique with the news while she was at the gym. Monique was shocked and unable to finish her workout.

Now, in prayer, she was determined to see change. She discerned the demonic activity at the intersection.

Monique: Lord! Why aren't there any other crashes on other streets? Why are there so many deaths at this one intersection? Something isn't adding up.

Holy Spirit: I have heard the people's cries. A blood covenant was made with darkness. Fast for seven days and gather the people to pray and walk through the community.

Monique: Lord, walk through the community? What would that look like?

Holy Spirit: Go to different churches and invite them. Get a police escort.

Monique wrapped up her prayer and went back to her double wide. She was able to purchase her home and land almost two years ago. She didn't think she could buy a home because she didn't have enough credit history; however, God favored her, and the company she purchased the property from went out of their way to get her into her dream home.

Monique had to get her mind together to do a seven day fast. She prepared a light meal and ate a Caesar salad with a cup of tomato bisque. She would start her fast in the morning, drinking only liquids.

Monique: I know God is trying to get something to me, so I will fast and pray.

The next morning, Monique's stomach grumbled. Her normal routine consisted of drinking coffee while consuming a blueberry bagel with cream cheese. However, she pushed past the hunger pains and drank a cup of herbal tea instead. She sat down at her kitchen table and opened the Bible. She read a couple of chapters, then went into prayer again.

Monique: Lord, give me strength to complete this seven day fast. I decree that no solid food will enter my mouth until this fast is completed.

As the days continued, she shut in. She didn't leave her home and withdrew from social media. Her only focus was God. Each day, Monique received revelation and could hear and feel God more. The first day of the fast seemed the hardest. Monique developed a headache as her body was flushing out the toxins. On day 3, she noticed that her tongue was coated. On day 5, her breath wasn't as fresh. Despite the physical changes, she experienced a spiritual difference. She felt God's fire consuming her deep within her bones as she prayed. She felt as if she had x-ray vision, gaining insight into the lives of those she interceded for.

On day 8, Monique woke up. She prayed and thanked God for strengthening her to complete the 7-day fast. She showered, got dressed, and made a cup of coffee. She was able to nibble on a bagel but didn't want to overdo it.

Monique: I have work to do.

Monique gets in her car and starts driving to different churches. When she pulls up to the first church, she prays before she gets out of the car.

Monique: Lord, help me to say the right thing.

Holy Spirit: Flow with me. I will give you the words to say.

Monique pressed past the nervousness, and God's boldness came upon her. She went inside the first church and stepped into the foyer.

Mother Boyd: Hello, young lady. Can I help you?

Mother Boyd was an elderly woman in her 70s. She dedicated her life to serving God and working at the church.

Monique: Yes, God led me here. My name is Monique Taylor. I'm a minister. God told me to ask if this church could partner with me to do a prayer walk in our community.

Mother Boyd: You know, we have been talking about doing some community events at some of our meetings. I will have to ask Pastor Miller. He is at the hospital visiting one of our members, but leave your contact information, and we will get back to you.

Monique smiled and handed Mother Boyd her business card. Then she left and drove to the next church. When she went into the next church, one of the deacons was vacuuming the sanctuary. The deacon stopped vacuuming when he saw Monique standing there, and Monique told the gentleman why she was there. The deacon took her card, and she left.

After Monique went to the fifth church, she felt discouraged because she had yet to receive a solid yes from any of the churches.

Monique: Lord, I know you didn't send me to all these churches for nothing.

Holy Spirit: Do what I told you.

Monique went to the police station and asked for a police escort for her event Saturday. She met Deputy Shannon Moore and discovered that she was also a Christian. Deputy Moore was glad to assist.

Monique went home to prepare a light lunch. As she was chopping up some lettuce, her phone rang. It was an administrator at one of the churches she visited. The lady on the other end of the phone informed her that the Bishop was interested and would like to get involved. Monique was delighted. She told the administrator that the prayer walk would be on Saturday morning.

By the end of the day, Monique heard from all five churches that she visited and they all said yes. They agreed to meet in the parking lot in front of the mall. Monique started praising God. Saturday was only five days away, so she went to the store to get a megaphone.

On Saturday at 7 a.m., Monique felt empowered, so she drove over to the mall. When she pulled up, she was amazed that the parking lot was already full. She got out of her car and waved at everyone. She got her megaphone out and instructed everyone to follow her. People exited their cars and walked over to the sidewalk in front of the store.

Monique: Good morning, everyone. My name is Monique Taylor. I'm a local minister here. Thank you for all gathering with me to help make a change in our community. God told me to do a seven day fast and to ask each of you to do a prayer walk. He ordered our steps to be here this day. I honor each of you in your respectful places, and the weapons of our warfare are not carnal but mighty through God for the pulling down of strongholds. This event is about Jesus and Him showing up mightily and overturning darkness. There have been too many deaths, especially at

5-Cross. Prayer changes things. We will begin walking in about 15 minutes to wait for those who may be running a little late. We will walk down to 5-Cross, going through the different neighbors, and then we will make our way back. We have Deputy Shannon Moore and her team escorting us today. Let's give the Lord a handclap for them.

The church crowd said amen as Monique spoke, and they clapped for the officers. More people came and it was time to walk. About 100 people cried out to God, making declarations for their community. Some spoke in tongues while others carried bottles of anointing oil, pouring it on every street they walked on. Some pleaded the blood of Jesus. One of the women said, "I command the spirit of death to cease and desist in Jesus' name." The police stopped traffic and ensured the group could safely cross the intersection at 5-Cross and make their way back to their cars.

While the saints prayed, Sonya Fuller felt a disruption in the spirit realm around her. She sat on her couch and felt an uneasiness come over her.

Sonya: What is happening?

Demon: People are praying.

Sonya: What! I must stop them.

Sonya quickly got dressed and rushed out of her apartment. She lived downtown by the mall, and as she stepped outside, she felt that the energy in her surroundings was different. She was upset and didn't like what was happening. She started jogging until she saw a crowd of people several yards ahead. However, that was the closest she could get. It was as if an invisible force was holding her back, and she could see a light around them.

Demon: You can't touch them. Go back.

Sonya knew the demon was right. The force and the light were too strong for her to penetrate. As she stared at the crowd walking, she noticed a lady in front with a megaphone.

Sonya: Who is that?

Demon: That's Monique Taylor. You are prohibited from touching her.

Sonya was full of rage and pride. She hoped that Monique Taylor would meet her demise. Sonya went back to her apartment, upset, and went into meditation. She wanted to change the energy around her.

Month after month went by and there were no accidents at 5-Cross. Sonya even went down to the intersection two more times, dropping goat blood and releasing death. Still, no accidents occurred. Sonya knew it was the Christians' prayers that stopped death from operating. Determined to bring Monique down, Sonya launched a smear campaign.

CHAPTER 3

How I Got My Power

The year was 1832, and Sonya's great-great-great-great grandmother, Hattie Johnson, sobbed from the depths of her soul. Hattie and other enslaved people were on the Johnson Plantation, witnessing as Willie Mays got whipped. The enslaved people were horrified, and they knew better than to intervene or speak out, or they would suffer the same fate. Willie Mays tried to escape because he heard about freedom in the North. However, after being missing for three days, Master Johnson hired slave catcher Mason Moore, who used bloodhounds to track down Willie Mays. The hounds tracked his scent to an old barn stored with hay on another's land. He had covered himself in the hay to rest during the day because he ran most of the night. Mason Moore returned Willie Mays to Master Johnson.

Horrified, exhausted, and bruised, Willie Mays endured lash after lash as his arms were stretched and bound to two poles. The agonizing beating felt like an eternity. Each time the wipe hit his back, his skin tore in several places. After Master Johnson was done, he had some slaves unleash Willie Mays's arms. Willie Mays dropped to the ground, weak, barely holding on to life. Some of the slaves took him inside his quarter to tend to his wounds and to provide him with nourishment.

Hattie Johnson was sick of Master's Johnson's treatment. She loved Willie Mays and wanted to be his wife, but as a slave, she wasn't allowed to marry. She was told that only free people could marry. However, in her mind, she and Willie Mays were married in God's sight. One day, while

Hattie was out in the field, she was summoned to the big house where the Master and his family lived. When she entered her Master's study room, Master Johnson instructed her to shut the door behind her. He told her to bend over the desk, but Hattie was resistant. Master Johnson overpowered Hattie, pushed her face into the desk with one hand, and lifted her slip with the other hand. He pulled out his genitals and raped her. With forceful thrusts, he penetrated her repeatedly. Hattie knew she couldn't scream or fight back. His wife and children were in the home and she knew it would infuriate her Master more if they heard her cry. Tears rolled down her eyes, and she laid there lifeless. Her mind shifted to childhood memories of her mother singing to cope with the pain. After the assault was over, Master Johnson fixed himself and his clothes, and he told Hattie, "Go on now. Get back to the fields."

Hattie fled from the big house and went far into the cotton fields to sob as she worked. She hated Master Johnson even more after he beat Willie Mays. She knew that if she wished harm on Master Johnson, he would soon meet his demise. She learned voodoo, a religion that originated in

West Africa that was brought to the Americas from some of the elder slaves. For weeks, after she finished working, she would make a doll out of wool stuffed with cotton. She would stick needles into the doll and say that the doll was Master Johnson. She was determined to avenge herself for the mistreatment. She took the doll into the graveyard at the edge of the plantation and buried and cursed it. "Master Johnson, you will get sick and die for all your evil." After she buried the doll, she spat on the grave.

One day, Master Johnson started to get a fever, and he got weaker throughout the week. Doctor Mullins was summoned and discovered that Master Johnson had milk sickness. He tried his best efforts to treat him but was unsuccessful. A week later, Master Johnson was dead. After his passing, his widow had to sell some of his assets to pay off his debt and moved away to her sister's home. Calvin Johnson, Master Johnson's brother, inherited the plantation and the slaves since he was the next of kin.

The new Master, Calvin Johnson, was much nicer. Hattie Johnson passed down her secret about what she had done to Master Johnson to the next generation. Sonya heard about her great-great-great-great grandmother Hattie and practiced some of the roots she was taught.

When Sonya was 5 years old, she told her mother, Carol, that a little girl in her classroom was mean to her.

Carol: What's the girl's full name?

Sonya: Jessica Jones.

Carol: I will take care of it.

The next day at school, all the children were at recess outside. Suddenly, there was a loud scream as Jessica sat on the ground holding her leg, crying. The teacher rushed to her side to find out what was happening, and Jessica told her that she had been stung by a bee. As a precaution, Jessica had to go to the nurse's office, and her parents were called.

When Sonya got home from school, she told her mom what happened.

Sonya: Mom. Guess what happened today?

Carol: What baby?

Sonya: Jessica got stung by a bee.

Carol: I may have played a part in that.

Sonya: Huh?

Carol: Baby, let me tell you about your great-great-great-great grandmother. In our family, we can make our enemies suffer. If someone does you wrong, they will pay a price.

Sonya didn't know how to feel. She listened and soaked up the information as a sponge. For many years, Carol taught Sonya the dark arts.

Carol kept a box in her bedroom closet. In the box was the knife she used to make animal sacrifices because she needed their blood to perform certain rituals. There were black candles to summon spirits and a mini coffin to hold different personalities. Sometimes, the coffin would be used to release a spirit of restlessness so the person could not sleep well at night.

The more Sonya heard and saw the strange objects her mother kept in the box and around the house, the more intrigued she became.

Carol: Let me tell you a story.

Carol and Sonya sat on the edge of the bed.

Carol: When you use this coffin, you must chant around it for 21 days. The number 21 in the kingdom of darkness means python. This spirit tricked Adam in the Garden of Eden. As a result, Adam fell and missed out on God's original plan for him. You can release the spirit of python, too. There are weak Christians who are easy to attack.

As the years went on, Carol showed Sonya how to release death, premature death, perversion, marital problems, financial problems, and sickness into people's lives.

Sometimes, they had to visit a cemetery to learn about demons. They would spend a night there and sleep on graves. A few times, they would dig up graves and get bones of people who died of cancer so they could release cancer on people. They would shave down the bones, put them in brown paper bags, and write people's names on them.

Another time, Carol showed Sonya how to contact marine spirits. When the ladies called on the devil and stayed up all night, a dark aura would appear. The demon would promise a reward for every successful task completed.

One time, a demon assigned them to shut down a church. The ladies took a black rooster, killed it, drank its blood, and then they cut the palms of their hands and drank their own blood. Sometimes, they would have to sleep on a bloody kitchen floor as demons would manifest themselves in their bodies. Through demonic power, they released the spirit of lust on the pastor, and in months, the pastor cheated on his wife, the congregation found out, and the church closed.

That night, $20,000 was deposited into Carol's account as their reward.

Carol and Sonya lived rent-free because every time their landlord came by or called to collect rent, he would forget or overlook them. He wasn't able to cross the threshold of their home. Demonic spirits altered his mind, causing him to forget and overlook their balance.

Sometimes, when the devil wanted to cause chaos in a church, these women would go visit during a service. They would leave rocks, feathers, sticks, or other objects behind on the floor or in the seats to release destruction on the members. As a result, some people would lose their jobs, commit suicide, or even miscarry.

One of their favorite assignments was to put people in jail. The ladies would visit different jails and gather dirt. Then, the individuals they targeted would spend several years in jail, sentenced for various crimes.

Carol taught her daughter how to curse a region because she felt that the people would be cursed if they could curse a region. She also taught her daughter how to do astral projection. Sometimes, the ladies would meet demons in the first and second heavens. Other times, they would go into people's homes and dreams.

One day, Carol developed a brain tumor and ended up passing away at the age of 53. She was unaware that those curses she released onto people came back on her. Sonya was devastated by the loss of her mom, and a spirit of bitterness and anger consumed her. She vowed in her heart to finish the work her mother started. However, she would soon discover a greater power for which she was no match.

CHAPTER 4

How I Got My Anointing

Monique Taylor was raised in a Southern Baptist church in McColl, South Carolina. Her parents are Eloise and Sherman, deacons and part of the committee board. Monique learned about God from her parents. They love the Lord and attend church every chance they could. Sometimes, they attended church four times a week. Most of the members are middle-aged or older, so Monique didn't have many kids her age to relate to in church. Monique quickly learned not to misbehave in the church —like falling asleep, putting her feet up on the pews, or horseplaying— because her mother would smack her quickly alongside her head in a way that no one seemed to notice. Her slap did the job, and Monique knew better, so she made sure she was on her best behavior.

She learned the basics of Christianity and had a good foundation in Sunday School. She learned about the Trinity, Jesus, salvation, baptism, and many Bible stories. However, Monique found herself getting bored and going through the motions. As she sat in church, she thought about the cutest boys in school, what she would eat when she got home, and what she would wear the next day at school.

At sixteen, Monique was blossoming into a beautiful young lady. Her breasts were tender from what seemed like an overnight growth spurt, and she had developed curves. Her straight figure was gone, and as she walked through the hallways at school, boys noticed her. One of the boys, Ricky, whom Monique had a crush on, became one of her suitors. Ricky was tall, had dark hair, was athletic, and had dimples.

He wrote a note with a heart emoji on the outside and slipped it into the vent slots in her locker. The note said: Dear Monique, This is Ricky Warren. I like you a lot and would like to know if you would go out with me. I hope you say yes. Ricky made sure he used Blue paper so his letter could stand out.

When the bell rang for the classes to change, Monique went to her locker to get her book for her next class. As she opened her locker, she noticed the blue paper folded up. She opened it and began to read it. When Monique saw the note, she blushed but maintained her cool in front of the other kids. She grabbed the note and her book and headed to her next class. As she sat in class, her mind wandered. "Oh wow. One of the cutest boys in school likes me."

During lunch, Monique ran into Ricky. The two sat beside each other and decided to become boyfriend and girlfriend. The two were inseparable. They would walk to class together, and whenever Monique could, she would sneak to call him even late on school nights. Her parents had no idea what was going on. On the outside, Monique seemed like she was on the right path. She attended church with her parents four times a week and made straight As. However, she was heading down the wrong path.

Monique and Ricky decided to skip school one day to take their relationship to the next level. Ricky's parents were at work and not home, so he invited Monique over. She didn't ride the school bus that morning. Ricky picked her up and took her to his house. When she got to his house, Ricky gave her a tour. They headed up to his room, and he showed her some of his football trophies.

The two sat down on his bed and started to kiss. Ricky laid her down and got on top of her. He began to caress her breasts and in between her thighs. Monique really liked Ricky and allowed him to continue.

Monique: Wait.

Ricky: What's wrong?

Monique: I never did this before.

Ricky: I love you.

She told him that she was a virgin, and he smiled. He kissed her further as a way to stop her from speaking. Ricky slipped off her underwear and penetrated her. The sexual experience lasted about 20 minutes. Monique had mixed feelings. The penetration hurt, but Ricky reassured her throughout that it was okay and that he would be gentle.

Afterward, the two went downstairs and made a frozen pizza. They ate, laughed, and watched TV for a little while. Now, it was time to head home because school was almost out. Ricky dropped Monique off around the corner from her home so she could pretend that she had ridden the bus.

A few days passed, Ricky seemed a little distant and didn't sit with Monique in the cafeteria. Someone told Monique that Ricky had been flirting with Cassandra, another classmate. Monique confronted Ricky about it, but he denied it, explaining that he sat with the football players because they asked him to that day.

While Monique was in class, she developed a deep itch in her vaginal canal. Unable to scratch and to avoid attention, she squeezed her vaginal muscles and wiggled a little in her chair. When the bell rang, Monique went to the restroom, and as she pulled down her underwear, she noticed a yellow discharge with a fishy smell. She tried to clean herself up as best as she could and endured the itch throughout the day.

Later, as she was heading to her next class, she saw Ricky standing too close to Cassandra's locker. When Ricky noticed Monique watching, his eyes widened - he knew he had been caught flirting. Monique asked to speak with him. The two walked down the hall, and Monique confronted him and decided to end things with him. She realized that he just used her, and once he got sex, he distanced himself. He lied about loving her. Hurt and itching, she just wanted to get through the day and go home. She couldn't wait to take a nice bubble bath.

When Monique got home, Ricky texted her.

Ricky: Hey, I'm sorry.

Monique: You lied about loving me.

Ricky: No, I didn't.

Monique: You just used me and lied about Cassandra.

Ricky: No I wasn't.

Ricky continued to deny everything. Monique couldn't worry about him anymore- she had to take care of herself.

Monique greeted her parents in the kitchen, and they told her to be ready by 6 p.m. so they could head to Bible study. Monique ran up the stairs and took a bubble bath. The bath seemed to provide some relief from the itch. However, the itching started again as Monique sat in church. The itch persisted so much as the night continued that Monique couldn't take it anymore.

She excused herself and went to the restroom to check things out. As she pulled down her panties, she saw more thick yellow discharge. She wiped it off her underwear with toilet paper, washed her hands, and returned to the sanctuary.

After service, when Monique and her parents returned home, Monique had to tell them what was going on. She was scared, but she needed help.

Monique: Mom. Dad. I need to tell you something.

Dad: Yes.

Both of her parents looked concerned. She wanted to hurry up and get it all out, so she blurted out what happened.

Monique: I had sex, and now I'm itching.

Both of her parents gasped, looking heartbroken.

Mom: You know better than that. We didn't raise you that way.

Dad: You probably contracted an STD.

Monique knew better than to say anything and feared what her parents would do next.

Mom: You are grounded. You are only allowed to go to school and come home straight. No phone or TV.

Dad: Where is the little boy you had sex with?

Monique: I broke things off with him because he was flirting with someone else.

Monique started to cry. Her father was upset, and he clenched his fists.

Mom: Give me all your devices. I'll take you to the clinic in the morning to get examined.

Monique felt a sense of relief now that everything was out in the open. The situation had gone better than she thought. She went upstairs and gave her parents her electronic devices. The net day, Monique and her mom went to the OB-GYN clinic. The nurse practitioner provided a pelvic exam and conducted an STD panel. Monique also had provide a urine sample.

Right away, the nurse was able to tell that Monique had an STD and decided to expedite the test so the results could be ready by the end of the day. She also provided some sex education, informing Monique about the ways to protect herself from STDs.

Later that evening, the clinic called, and Monique's mom was informed that Monique had trichomoniasis and chlamydia. They went to the pharmacy to pick up the prescribed medication, and the clinic scheduled a follow-up appointment to ensure the infection cleared up.

The next day at school, Monique pulled Ricky aside and told him that he had given her trichomoniasis and chlamydia and that he needed to be checked out. He denied giving it to her. Monique reminded him that she was a virgin when they had sex and that she had never been with anyone else. Then she walked away.

As weeks passed, Monique rededicated her life to Jesus Christ. She felt foolish because she gave her virginity away to someone who didn't deserve it. Ricky had proved to be a compulsive liar. Monique learned in church that when you fall into sin, nothing good comes out of it. Marriage was supposed to be special and honorable in God's sight. She vowed to remain celibate until marriage. Initially, she was upset that her first experience with sex resulted in STDs, but with God's help, she moved past it. She knew God forgave her and didn't condemn her.

Monique remained grounded for the rest of 10th grade and most of the 11th grade. Her parents finally lifted her punishment during spring break. Monique was so happy but didn't want to use her freedom to sin. When her devices were returned, she went on YouTube and saw someone pushing a lady to the altar in a wheelchair to get prayer. After the lady received prayer, she was able to get out of the wheelchair and walk for the first time in years. As she started walking, the church exploded in praise unto God. Evangelist Washington was the woman who prayed for the wheelchair-bound woman.

Monique had never seen anyone get healed and had only read about healing in the Bible. At her church, no one had ever been healed. She wanted to learn more and started watching Evangelist Washington's videos. She learned about the supernatural, prophecy, the word of knowledge, and the word of wisdom. All these things were foreign to her; she desired them because Evangelist Washington taught her that the Holy Spirit gives gifts to those who ask.

Monique discovered that Evangelist Washington was coming to her town in a couple of weeks. She got permission from her parents to attend the revival meeting. She was determined to stay focused in school and on the deeper things of God.

On the night of the revival service, the glory of God was so strong on Evangelist Washington. When she spoke, it was as the scriptures say, with authority, like when Jesus spoke. Every word that Evangelist Washington said seemed to go through Monique's body, and she started to feel very hot. She didn't understand what was happening and felt the fire of God.

People couldn't get close to Evangelist Washington without falling. Monique was stunned and didn't understand everything but knew it was God. Evangelist Washington supernaturally knew that someone in the crowd had a lump on their arm.

Evangelist Washington: The Holy Spirit gave me a word of knowledge that someone here has a lump on your arm. Come to the altar.

A lady came to the altar wearing a blazer, but as she removed it, a baseball-sized lump was visible on her forearm. The crowd was amazed.

Evangelist Washington: In the name of Jesus, I command this lump to dissolve by the fire of God."

Miraculously, before everyone's eyes, the lump disappeared. The crowd started praising Jesus, and the woman wept and fell out under God's power.

Evangelist Washington then started moving around the room, and as she laid her hand on people, they began falling out. When Evangelist Washington touched Monique, she fell back, and someone caught her and put a sheet over her. While she was down on the floor, she saw a big bright angel standing in front of her. The angel's wing span touched from one side of the room to the other. He stood over 12 feet tall, glowing with a light unlike anything Monique had ever seen. The angel had four faces: one of a man, a lion, an ox, and an eagle. He carried a long, glistening sword. As the angel walked through the room, the people fell. The vision seemed so real. When she opened her eyes and began to move, two ladies helped her off the floor, and she went back to her seat but couldn't stop shaking. She had no idea that she had just received an impartation.

When she arrived home, she shared everything she experienced with her parents. They seemed indifferent and had no desire to experience that level of glory for themselves. That night, as she laid in the bed, she heard the voice of God call out to her:

Holy Spirit: I am thy Lord thy God. I will use you for My glory. You will flow in miracles and teach people about righteousness.

Monique started to weep because she could feel God's tangible presence and couldn't stop trembling. Warmth covered her entire body. She couldn't believe how real God was and that He chose to speak to her. Had she known God like this before, she would have never backslid.

As the year went by, Monique drew closer to God and discovered her purpose. Growing up, she had experienced demonic nightmares and learned to call on Jesus to pray them away. But now, Monique knew that Jesus was more than just a name to call on for relief from nightmares—she knew His Holy Spirit and developed a relationship with Him.

One day, the Holy Spirit told Monique to attend a prophetic school where they activated and taught about the prophetic ministry. She attended the three-day event and felt more confident in her ability to prophesy. Afterward, she reached another level spiritually. God would sometimes instruct her to walk up to random people in the grocery store and prophesy to them.

Monique prophesied to most of her classmates in college and told everyone she could about Jesus Christ. After graduating with a degree in political science, she moved out of her parent's home into her own apartment. Every two weeks, on her night off from work, she would go on social media to do a live video ministering to people.

One night, on a live video, a lady asked for prayer. As Monique started to pray for the lady, she saw a calendar in the spirit realm.

Monique: I see a calendar come before me, and a date is circled as September 12th. Does that mean anything?

Lady: Umm. Noo..Umm..yes! I just remembered that I have an appointment that day. They are trying to tell me something bad.

Monique: Really?

Lady: Yeah, cancer.

Monique: Well, we bind that up right now in the name of Jesus!

Lady: Amen.

At that moment, Monique started to get a throbbing pain in her left breast.

Monique: Do you have any throbbing pain in your left breast? I'm asking because sometimes God allows me to feel the pain of the person I'm praying for.

Lady: Yes. I found a lump in that breast.

Monique: Can you feel the lump now?

Lady: Yes.

Monique: What size is the lump?

Lady: It's about the size of a quarter.

Monique: Okay, well, the Holy Spirit is highlighting this area, so He wants you to be healed tonight. So, in the name of Jesus, I command this lump to dissolve by fire. I command the lump to go right now in Jesus' mighty name. Now check for the lump.

The lady starts searching and pressing down on her breasts; her eyes widen in shock, and she started crying.

Lady: Oh my God! Oh God! It's gone. I can't find it.

Monique: What?

Monique couldn't believe her ears. She knew that God was a healer, but she never thought He would use her in this capacity.

Lady: It's gone!

At that moment, Monique fell to her knees, wept, and praised God!

Monique: Wow! Hallelujah!

The viewers on the broadcast were all praising God as well.

A few months later, God instructed Monique to have a gathering in her area. She stepped out in faith, nervous that no one would come. She didn't know where the money would come from to pay for everything, but God sent so many people to donate toward the conference. On the night of the event, the room was full of people who traveled from out of town. The anticipation in the atmosphere was palpable as God's presence filled the room.

During the conference, the Holy Spirit gave Monique a word of knowledge. In an internal conversation, the Holy Spirit whispered, "There is someone here with a leg shorter than the other, and I want you to call it out."

Monique replied, "God, really? There doesn't seem to be anyone here that fits that description."

The Holy Spirit gently responded, "Trust me."

Monique gripped the microphone and spoke what God had told her.

Monique: The Holy Spirit said someone here has one leg shorter than the other.

As Monique looks at the crowd, a young lady approaches the altar.

Young girl: That's me. I have sclerosis and sometimes I have back pain.

Monique: Okay, have a seat in this chair.

Monique pulled a chair forward and the young lady sat. Monique got on her knees and instructed the lady to put her legs together and hold them out. Monique held her legs up and measures them, seeing that the left leg was 1 ½ inch shorter than the right leg. Everyone in the crowd saw the differences in the length as well. The young lady, though hopeful, was still skeptical about what was to come.

Monique: I command this leg to grow out in Jesus' name to match the length of the other leg.

At that moment, Monique felt the foot shoot out as she held it in her hand. The young lady's face was a mix of shock and awe as she saw what God had just done. She began to weep as she saw that her two legs were now even. The crowd erupted with praise and they talked about all the miracles they witnessed.

Monique was in awe of God and stayed humble as God entrusted her with some of the deepest secrets of those around her. As the year was ending, God instructed Monique to host an online meeting and minister to His people. The spirit of prophecy was strong on the call, and Monique began taking prayer requests.

Christina: Hello. My name is Christina Bowles, and I'm battling depression. I just need God to move in my life.

Monique: Nice to meet you, Christina. I'm sorry that you are going through a tough time. God will give you beauty for ashes.

As Monique started to pray, she felt as if her chest was caving in.

Monique: Are you having chest pains? I feel like my chest is caving in. It's deep in my ribcage.

Christina: Yes. I have a hard time breathing sometimes.

Monique: Well, you will be healed tonight in Jesus' name. I command the spirit of infirmity to go in Jesus' name.

At that moment, Monique's spiritual eyes opened, and she began to see the source of Christina's pain. She saw a little imp around 3 feet tall that resembled a short black woman. Its skin was dark, and it had curly white hair. However, its face was distorted, twisted to the side. Its eyes were large and black with no iris. It's teeth were sharp and the imp seemed to be floating.

The demon tried to taunt Monique when it realized she could see it. Monique prayed fervently until she saw the demon leave and an angel arrive.

Monique: I rebuked the demonic spirit of depression and sickness in Jesus' name.

Christiana took a deep sigh as she could now breathe better.

Monique: How do you feel? I don't feel the pain in my chest anymore. Do you?

Christiana: I feel great. Glory to God! Whew! I can breathe better. Wow.

Monique: Amen. God is so good. Let's all give God praise for what He has done tonight. Be in expectation. I pray blessings over you and I will see you all next time.

Monique was shaken up because she had never seen a demon as she prayed for someone. The demon had tried to jump at her in the realm of the spirit as she prayed, but she stood her ground and prayed harder. She had to end the call earlier than usual because she couldn't believe what had just happened. After Monique ended the broadcast, she went into her room and prayed.

Monique: God, what was that?

Holy Spirit: Get used to it. I am making you My battle ax and My weapon of war.

Monique showered and decided to call it a night. She thought about what the Holy Spirit said, "Get used to it." She wasn't looking forward to seeing demons or dealing with them. However, the Holy Spirit proved to be right because, over the next couple of months, she would encounter many dark forces who sought to destroy her.

CHAPTER 5

The Battle Begins

Sonya woke up early with vengeance on her mind. She hated the fact that Christians had marched through the community, praying and disrupting the atmosphere. She craved more power to become a high-ranking priestess, and she needed blood.

She got on her computer and began to search various social media platforms for Monique

Taylor. She looked at her photos, read her posts, and watched her videos. Sonya wanted to get a feel for who was behind the prayer meeting. She saved a photo of Monique and began summoning demonic energy. Full of pride, she ignored the demon's warning not to touch Monique. Sonya believed she ranked higher in the spirit and was more powerful.

She ordered the demons to cause sickness in Monique's life.

Sonya: Make her suffer failures in business and at work. Cause many enemies and envious people to attack her. Let her be surrounded only by rejection and hostility.

After Sonya finished, she smiled, considering herself a professional spellcaster.

Sonya: Now all I have to do is sit back and wait.

On the other side of town, Monique woke up with a headache. She had felt the pain in her sleep, and its throbbing intensity caused her to awaken. Monique sat up in bed, rubbing her temples. She carefully went to the restroom to get ready for her day knowing sudden movements would worsen the pain. From her medicine cabinet, she took two Excedrin pills, brushed her teeth, and showered as gently as possible. Still in pain, she prayed.

Monique: I rebuke this headache in Jesus' name.

A half-hour later, the pain let up. Monique got dressed and headed to the city council meeting. When she arrived, she noticed that some people who usually were friendly were now cold towards her. She waved and smiled before the meeting began, but it seemed no one wanted to greet her.

Monique began to think to herself, "Hmm, this is weird. Did I do something to offend everyone?"

After the meeting was over, Monique saw Susan in the hall. She called her name and walked up to her, happy to see her.

Monique: Hey Susan. Hey girl. How are you?

Susan looked upset and flabbergasted.

Susan: Are you seriously talking me to right now?

Monique: Huh?

Susan: You have some nerve.

Monique: I'm sorry. Did I do something wrong?

Susan: I saw your post. You wrote that status about me.

Monique: What?

Monique was confused. She had no idea what Susan was referring to.

Susan: The post about operating in fear. You knew my situation and what you wrote made me feel like cramp.

Monique: Sis, come on. I would never post anything about you. I value our friendship. As I recall, I posted a scripture and did commentary about it but I can assure you, the post had nothing to do with you.

Susan: Yeah right.

Susan smacked her teeth, rolled her eyes, and walked away. Monique stood in the hallway, dumbfounded. She couldn't believe what had happened. She pulled out her phone and went on social media to find out why Susan was so upset.

Social media post:
"2 Timothy 1:7, 'For God hath not given us the spirit of fear; but of power, and of love, and of a sound mind.'

"Many of us have allowed fear to hold us back. We make up excuses why we can't do something. We allow fear to cause us to disobey God. Fear has caused sickness and stumbling blocks in our lives. We are afraid to preach, meet new people, get out of our comfort zones, and step into the deep. Get delivered today from fear."

Monique reread the post a few more times, trying to figure out how Susan could possibly feel this status was for her. She was bothered and felt a little sad. She remembered the Bible verse that said that God is not the author of confusion, so she knew somehow the devil was influencing Susan's mind.

Monique went to her favorite deli for a panini and a side salad. She sat on the patio outside the restaurant, scrolling through social media and eating lunch. Suddenly, she came across a blog post about her.

Warning! Watch Out For Charismatic Charlatan Monique Taylor!

The article claimed that Monique was a false teacher, summoned demonic powers to assist her, and that she was leading many people astray with her damnable heresies. Reading this post really upset Monique.

"Wow! This is all lies! All I do is serve and love people. I always try my best to encourage others," she thought.

Immediately, she regretted reading the article. "Ugh, why did I allow this negativity in my spirit?" she thought. She lost her appetite, boxed up her food, and pushed past the discouragement. She then drove to Lake View Park to seek peace. She knew that the article was untrue, and she didn't even know the person who wrote it. As she sat in the car, staring at the lake, and pondering the article, a sharp stabbing pain went into her back. It felt like needles were sticking into her skin.

Monique: Ouch! God, what is going on?

Holy Spirit: Witchcraft!

Monique: What!

Holy Spirit: Use the authority that Jesus gave. Fast and pray.

Monique couldn't believe what she heard. Righteous indignation came upon her, and she began to pray fervently.

Monique: In the name of Jesus, I bind up witchcraft. Lord, you said, "Suffer not a witch to live." I break witchcraft off my mind, body, will, and emotions. I break witchcraft off my family, friends, and ministry. I break witchcraft off my business and finances. I plead the blood of Jesus Christ and pray a thick wall of fire around me. I decree that no weapon formed against me shall prosper in the name of Jesus.

Then she prayed hard in tongues or her heavenly language for several minutes until she felt relieved. She couldn't believe she was going through a demonic attack. She knew it had to be the spirit of backlash or retaliation for doing the prayer march. She sat in the car for a little while longer, waiting to see if the Holy Spirit would say anything else, and then she drove back to her house.

Across town, Sonya sat on her balcony and enjoying the view of the city. Suddenly, she felt nauseous and ran to the restroom to vomit. . Her head began to pound, the room spun, and she clutched the toilet bowl for balance as her stomach churned.

A few minutes later, Sonya emerged from the restroom and went into her kitchen to grab a few saltines. The demonic spirit manifested before her as she was nibbling on the cracker.

Demon: There is a law of reciprocity. You must get stronger.

Sonya knew the demon was right, so for the next several weeks, she focused on weaker Christians or those who were lukewarm. She targeted people who partied in the club on Friday and went to church on Sunday. She needed to collect their soul.

Darius Green grew up in church, but his heart was far from God. He didn't read his Bible or maintain an active prayer life. He attended church out of routine and to dress to impress. He was looking for a wife, even if she wasn't a godly woman. Darius loved R&B and secular music and went to Club Passion every Friday.

One night, after a long day at work, Darius came home feeling exhausted and hungry. He warmed up some leftover fettuccine from a popular Italian restaurant, watched some football commentary, and then went to bed.

As he laid in bed, he drifted off to sleep only to be awaken an hour later by a thick presence of evil. He was half asleep and awake at the same time. Each time he tried to drift off to sleep, he felt paralyzed, unable to breathe. Terrified, he wiggled free and sat up, panting and afraid. He quickly turned on the lights. With heavy sleep in his eyes, he knew he had to pray. He cried out to Jesus for help.

Darius didn't realize that Sonya had astral projected into his room on a mission to snatch his soul. As he prayed and repented for his sins, an angel arrived, bringing a bright light that surrounded Darius. Sonya knew she could no longer touch Darius, so she fled back to the spirit realm to find another victim.

Sonya didn't have to look far. Next door, Kirsten Young laid fast asleep. Kirsten had backslidden and hadn't attended church in years. She was obsessed with being a beauty influencer and growing her social media following. She spent hours at the gym sculpting her "Coke bottle" figure.

Sonya entered Kirsten's room and held her down. Struggling to free herself, Kirsten awoken in a frozen state of fear. She was mute, and no matter how hard she tried, she couldn't speak. She felt like she was suffocating. Kirsten tried for several minutes to move, but she was exhausted and completely paralyzed. Sonya held her down with all her strength each time Kirsten tried to wiggle herself free.

Kirsten couldn't see Sonya but could sense an evil presence in her bedroom. Finally, after one last attempt to escape, Kirsten felt her breath leave her body, and her soul was snatched.

Sonya returned to her body, holding the silver cord that tethered her soul. When she returned, a dark aura appeared as a demon manifested.

Demon: Thank you for another soul. I am giving you the strength of ten more demons.

Sonya was pleased. She wanted supernatural strength because she wanted to travel the world and be sought out as a high-ranking priestess. Her next goal was to cause more bloodshed in her community. She performed another ritual at a nearby road, hoping to provoke accidents, but weeks passed without any incidents.

Frustration grew and she knew Monique was the reason. Sonya felt empowered and like she was strong enough to take out Monique. One night, at 3 a.m., she astral projected into Monique's bedroom. Monique was asleep. She watched Monique's chest rise and fall as she slept. Hatred filled her, and she reached into Monique's chest cavity to grab her soul.

Suddenly, Monique's eyes flew open, and Sonya realized that Monique could see her. Panic hit her, and she let go. Monique's soul snapped back into her body like a rubber band.

Monique: Ouch!

Sonya disappeared and fled back into her body. She was shaken. "How could Monique see me?" She thought. Now, she would be able to identify her in person. She thought, "Usually, people can't see me in the spirit."

Monique sat up in bed, her heart racing. She had felt the evil presence in her room. and tried to process what had just happened. She felt internal pain from where her soul was trying to be snatched. It actually felt like she had been popped with a rubber band. She was upset and felt violated.

Immediately, she went into prayer. She rebuked every spirit she could think of and prayed until she felt the evil presence leave and God's peace upon her. Though she felt calmer, she felt shaken. She couldn't believe she had seen the woman who attacked her. The details of Sonya's curly hair and brown complexion were vivid in her mind. It was the first time a witch had ever astral projected into her room.

After an hour of prayer, she felt secure enough to go back to sleep. When she woke up, she sat on her couch, ready to hear from the Holy Spirit.

Holy Spirit: Her name is Sonya Fuller, and she lives downtown in Patriot Apartments.

"What?" Monique thought to herself. "How did she find me? What did I ever do to her? She tried to kill me."

So many thoughts rushed through Monique's mind. She went on social media to look up the name that the Holy Spirit had given her. Sure enough, there was the lady who was standing over her last night. As she stared at Sonya's profile photo, her mouth dropped in shock. She knew that in the Bible God had told Elisha the very words the King spoke in his private bed chamber, but to receive inside information herself blew her mind.

Monique now understood the source of all the chaos in her city, the wicked blog post, and her falling out with Susan. "I can't believe a witch is harassing me," she said, shaking her head in disapproval.

Immediately, Monique picked up her phone and dialed her spiritual mother, Jessica Edwards.

Prophetess Edwards was a seasoned saint who served on the intercession team at her church. Although she lived in another state, Monique called her every few weeks for advice and prayer.

Prophetess Edwards: Hello.

Monique: Hey, Mom.

Prophetess Edwards: Hey, sugar. How are you?

Monique: Well, I am going through some warfare. Last night, a witch astral projected into my room.

Prophetess Edwards: We bind up this now in Jesus' name and plead the blood of Jesus.

Monique: The Holy Spirit gave me her name, and I looked her up on social media, and it was her.

Prophetess Edwards: Did you cut the silver cord?

Monique: No. What's that?

Prophetess Edwards: The Book of Ecclesiastes tells us that when we cut the silver cord, the body returns to dust. Witches use that cord to return to their bodies when they travel in the spirit. If you cut it, then they will die because they can't make their way back.

Monique: Wow!

Prophetess Edwards: Come on, baby, let's bombard heaven and go to the throne of grace.

The two women prayed and God's presence met them where they were. After they finished praying, they chatted for a little while before disconnecting. Monique knew she was a target to the enemy, so she decided to fast for God's protection and commit to praying without ceasing.

Across town, Sonya sat on her balcony when a loud noise like thunder erupted beside her head. She felt pain in her body and the demonic energy around her was disrupted.

Sonya: Whoah! Ah! What's happening?

Demon: Prayers of attack are being launched at you.

Sonya ran inside and ducked for cover in the hall closet. Every prayer sent felt like torture, leaving her in agony. A little while later, she felt beaten and drained. Remembering the demon's warning about the law of reciprocity, she vowed to get stronger. But for now, she knew she needed to rest.

The next day, Sonya went on social media and saw that Monique was having a conference in three months. She planned to attend and take Monique out once and for all. Over the following weeks, Sonya prepared herself through fasting, rituals, and making more blood sacrifices. She was determined to grow in power for the confrontation.

Across town, Monique attended the monthly town hall meetings. After the meeting ended, Susan approached her.

Susan: Monique, wait.

Monique stopped walking and turned around, seeing Susan approaching her.

Susan: I am so sorry for how I treated you. God showed me it was the enemy. The devil wanted me to come against you. In prayer, God delivered me and showed me the error of my ways. Can you forgive me?

Monique: Oh, of course.

The two women hugged.

Susan: You were right about what you posted. I was allowing fear to hold me back from doing what God called me to do, and I got offended. Offense is something I struggle with, but God is working on me.

Monique: I love you, sis, and I want the best for you. I will never judge you. When you became upset with me, it hurt me, but I went to God and truly forgave you.

Susan: Aww, I bless God for you. What are you about to do? Can we go to Joe's Deli to catch up?

Monique: Absolutely.

The women drove to the Deli and ordered lunch. Over the hot meal, they chatted about everything happening in each other's lives. Monique told Susan about the witchcraft attacks. Susan vowed to become a better friend and pray for Monique more.

A few weeks later, the conference was just one month away. Monique promoted it on her social media networks, and people were excited to attend. She needed some prayer warriors to stand with her to prepare, so she asked Prophetess Edwards and Susan to do a 21-day fast with her and to pray over the conference. Every night at 6:30 pm, these ladies met on a conference call and prayed various prayer points. They declared God's protection over the event and prayed for God's glory to fall upon those in attendance.

As the event drew closer, God's fire rested heavily upon Monique. She felt reassured that

His presence was guiding her. She felt renewed and could hear from the Holy Spirit on a deeper level.

Meanwhile, across town, Sonya had also been preparing. For 21 days, she meditated on her desires for Monique downfall. She surrounded herself with black candles, drew a pentagram on her floor, and placed Monique's photo in the center.

The day of the conference had arrived. Monique had rented out a ballroom at Hilton Head Hotel. She and other women gathered to decorate the venue early on the day of the conference and pray over every chair. They anointed every corner of the ballroom with oil.

That night, the people arrived with great expectancy, packing the room. The hotel staff heard people praising God and came to check out the service. They couldn't stay long, but they felt God's presence. There was a tangible fire that could be felt in the parking lot all the way to the reception desk.

Sonya checked the time and made her way down to the Hilton Head Hotel. She was surprised by how full the parking lot was and managed to find a spot near the dumpsters. As she got out of her vehicle, a warm sensation swept over her, making her uneasy. Her eyes began to water, but she pressed forward, determined to confront Monique.

Every step felt like a struggle. She entered the ballroom, and her eyes burned as tears poured down her face. Sonya found a seat in the back of the room, disgusted by everything she saw. She noticed that she wasn't the only one crying. Her tears were tears of pain while others seemed to be tears of joy and freedom.

Sonya sat through the service, watching Monique and the other ladies speak. When Monique took the stage, she received words of knowledge and began calling people out.

Monique: There is someone here who got in a car accident, hurt your right shoulder, and the pain keeps flaring up. Please come forth so I can pray for you.

A woman in her mid-fifties stood up and made her way towards the front of the room. As soon as the lady got close to Monique, she fell backward. Some of the women quickly caught her before she hit the ground and covered her with a modesty blanket. She had been slain in the spirit.

As the lady laid on the ground, Sonya began chanting out loud. Some people sitting near her noticed though the loud music at the front of the room made it hard for Monique to hear the chants.

Sonya: I call upon the spirits of 29570.

She repeated this phrase while writing down the names of people Monique called out in a yellow notebook. As some of the attendees around her began to pray in tongues, Sonya became irritated. She didn't know how much longer she could stay in the service. Her eyes burned, her body felt hot, and the praises of the people sounded like flies buzzing in her ears.

Sonya finally decided she had had enough. She began to gather herself to charge toward Monique.

After Monique finished praying for the lady who hurt her shoulder in the car accident, the Holy Spirit spoke to her.

Holy Spirit: The witch is here.

Monique: What do you want me to do?

Holy Spirit: Get a trash can and some paper towels.

Monique paused, momentarily confused, then turned to Malcolm, one of the volunteer ushers standing near the door.

Monique: Malcolm, can you please get me a trash can and paper towels?

Malcolm hurried to the back of the room, returning moments later with the items. Monique continued her internal conversation with the Holy Spirit.

Monique: What do I do?

Holy Spirit: Call her out and follow My unction.

Monique stepped to the microphone and instructed everyone to have a seat and to pray in their heavenly language for 30 seconds.

Monique: Sonya Fuller, come here? I know you are in this room.

Sonya froze in her seat, uncomfortable and shocked that Monique knew her name. She reluctantly got up, but every step felt like she was carrying heavy weights. Tears streamed down her face, soaking her blouse as she made her way to the front of the room. Her eyes locked with Monique's.

Sonya didn't realize she was experiencing the glory of God. She only felt pain and confusion, unable to process what was happening.

Monique felt a supernatural boldness come upon her.

Monique: I know you came here to hurt me, but no weapon formed against me will prosper in Jesus' name.

At that moment, Sonya let out a growl. She summoned all her energy and rushed forward, attempting to tackle Monique. She was able to speed up some, but she was not fast enough.

Monique: I loose the fire of God upon you right now in Jesus Christ's name! Fire! Fire! The Fire of the Holy Ghost!

Every time Monique said "fire," Sonya screamed in pain. It felt like Sonya's skin was peeling off. She let out a blood-curdling scream and fell forward, frozen in place as the demonic spirits within her came to the surface. Her body wiggled like a snake. The attendees sprang into action. Some stretched out their hands towards her, fervently praying. Some prayed in tongues, while others were binding and rebuking the devil.

Suddenly, Sonya began to gag. She turned her head to the side. Deaconess Brown rushed to her side with the paper towels and the trash can as the thick, white, frothy foam emerged. Sonya continued purging, coughing, and gagging, as the people around her worshipped God.

The worship team led the congregation in song, creating an atmosphere of deliverance. The power of God filled the room as Sonya continued to vomit into the trash can. The spirit of hatred, along with other demonic forces, began to leave her body one by one.

When the deliverance was complete, Sonya came to her senses. Disoriented, she stood up with help. Overwhelmed with shame, Sonya rushed out of the building, leaving her yellow notebook behind.

She got into her car and tried to start it, but it wouldn't turn over. Embarrassed, confused, and unsure of her next move, she sat in the driver's seat, tears streaming down her face. She remembered the demon's warning weeks earlier: "Do not touch Monique because there was a light around her."

"I let selfish ambition guide my steps. What have I done?" she thought to herself.

For the first time, Sonya doubted her ability to finish what her mother had started. She felt defeated and unsure of her next move.

Meanwhile, inside the conference, the attendees praised God for what they had witnessed. They rejoiced that a witch had received deliverance and that God had protected everyone. Their voices rose in unison as they prayed:

Dear Heavenly Father,

We lift up Sonya Fuller and others operating in witchcraft. We pray for complete deliverance and salvation. Draw her closer to you, Lord. Get every spirit out of her that is not of you. Lord, send forth the fire of the Holy Ghost to touch her wherever she is. Let her repent, be saved, and turn from her wicked ways in Jesus Christ's name. Amen.

After the prayer, Monique addressed the crowd. She shared the warfare she had faced, including Sonya's astral projection into her room.

She encouraged everyone not to fear but to use the authority of Jesus Christ in their daily lives.

Monique: Always remember, the weapons of our warfare are not carnal but mighty through God for the pulling down of strongholds. Live holy lives, and don't let the enemy intimidate you. Remember, Sonya is a lost soul. The Holy Spirit, in His love and mercy, wants her to be saved.

Back in the car, Sonya wept uncontrollably. She could feel God's presence all around her, yet she felt trapped in a battle between light and darkness. Pounding the steering wheel in frustration, she screamed.

"I've reached the end of myself. My power is no match for Jesus," she yelled out loud.

Sonya realized this was the beginning of her journey to deliverance. Little did she know, the very spirits she had once allied with would now turn against her.

Salvation

I pray that this story of the prophet versus the witch touched you and warned you about the dangers of witchcraft. The flesh profits no good thing (John 6:63), and sin equals death (Romans 6:23). No matter how deep you are into witchcraft, Jesus Christ can set you free. Try Him today and allow His Holy Spirit to guide you into divine freedom. Experience His love and peace. He's only a prayer away. Say this prayer and allow Him to enter your heart.

Romas 10:9 says that if I confess with my mouth and believe in my heart, I will be saved. I want to make you Lord of my life. Come into my heart and deliver me from the works of the flesh, witchcraft, voodoo, magic, and other dark arts. I renounce Satan and confess that Jesus Christ is Lord. I will step out in faith and throw anything away that will tie me to the devil or allow the devil to have access to me. Lead me to a Bible-based church and strengthen me. Thank you for answering this prayer in Jesus Christ's name.

About The Author

Kimberly Moses started off her ministry as Kimberly Hargraves. She is highly sought after as a prophetic voice, intercessor and prolific author. There is no doubt that she has a global mandate on her life to serve the nations of the world by spreading the Gospel of Jesus Christ. She has a quickly expanding worldwide healing and deliverance ministry. Kimberly Moses wears many hats to fulfill the call God has placed on her life as an entrepreneur over several businesses including her own personal brand Rejoice Essentials which promotes the Gospel of Jesus Christ.

She also serves as a life coach and mentor to many women. She is also the loving mother of two wonderful children. She is married to Tron. Kimberly has dedicated her life to the work of ministry and to serve others under the call God has placed over her life. Kimberly currently resides in South Carolina.

She is a very anointed woman of God who signs, miracles and wonders follow. The miraculous and incessant testimonies attributed to her ministry are incalculable, with many reporting physical and mental healing, financial breakthroughs, debt cancellations and other favorable outcomes. She is known across the globe as a servant who truly labors on behalf of God's people through intercession.

She is the author of The Following:

"Overcoming Difficult Life Experiences with Scriptures and Prayers"
"Overcoming Emotions with Prayers"
"Daily Prayers That Bring Changes"

"In Right Standing,"
"Obedience Is Key,"
"Prayers That Break The Yoke Of The Enemy: A Book Of Declarations,"
"Prayers That Demolish Demonic Strongholds: A Book Of Declarations,"
"Work Smarter. Not Harder. A Book Of Declarations For The Workforce,"
"Set The Captives Free: A Book Of Deliverance."
"Pray More Challenge"
"Walk By Faith: A Daily Devotional"
"Empowering The New Me: Fifty Tips To Becoming A Godly Woman"
"School of the Prophets: A Curriculum For Success"
"8 Keys To Accessing The Supernatural"
"Conquering The Mind: A Daily Devotional"
"Enhancing The Prophetic In You"
"The ABCs of The Prophetic: Prophetic Characteristics"
"Wisdom Is The Principal Thing: A Daily Devotional"
"It Cost Me Everything"
"The Making Of A Prophet: Women Walking in Prophetic Destiny"
"The Art of Meditation: A Daily Devotional"

"Warfare Strategies: Biblical Weapons"
"Becoming A Better You"
"I Almost Died"
"The Pastor's Secret: The D.L. Series"
"June Bug The Busy Bee: The Gamer"
"June Bug The Busy Bee: The Bully"
"The Weary Prophet: Providing Practical Steps For Restoration"
"The Insignificant Woman"
"The Foolish Woman: A Daily Devotional"
"June Bug The Busy Bee: Sibling Rivalry"
"All Things Relationships"
"30 Day Pray For Your Spouse Challenge"
"The Christian Drama Queen Mentality"
"30 Days Praying For The Nations"
"Intercessor's Prayer Notebook"
"Prayer Request Notebook Fervent Effectual Prayers Of The Righteous"
"The Prophet's Notebook"
"The Photographer's Assistant"
"The Ultimate Entrepreneur"
"Diabetic Caretaker Blood Sugar Log"
"The Preacher's Handbook"
"Christian Weight Loss Journal"
"Couple's Recipe Meal Planner And Notebook"
"Prophetic Dreams And Visions Journal"

"The Therapist Secret: The D.L. Series"
"Tabuletta"
"Tested, Tried, But I Survived"
"The Wounded Leader: Deliverance And Healing From The Aftermath of Trauma"
"Walking In His Peace: A Daily Devotional"

You can find more about Kimberly at www.kimberlyhargraves.com

For Rejoice Essential Magazine, visit www.rejoiceessential.com

For beauty, hair, and t-shirts, visit www.rejoicingbeauty.com

Please write a review for my books on Amazon.com

Support this ministry:
Cashapp: $ProphetKimberlyMoses
Paypal.me/remag
Venmo: Kimberly-Moses-19

Follow my YouTube Channels:
Kimberly Moses

Kimberly Finds
The Moses Agency
Scams Plots Schemes

Follow my music journey by looking up "Prophetess K" on all streaming platforms.

www.ingramcontent.com/pod-product-compliance
Lightning Source LLC
LaVergne TN
LVHW051956060526
838201LV00059B/3682